A COLLECTION OF MICROLIT

SPECULATE

EUGEN BACON

DOMINIQUE HECQ

Meerkat Press
Asheville

Contents

in lieu of a preface

by Dominique Hecq and Eugen Bacon

This book began as a dialogue between two adventurous writers curious about the shapeshifter we call a prose poem, that can be the hybrid of a poem and a flash fiction. Aware of our penchants and differentiations, we pushed ourselves to detach from each of our safe zones—for one, it was speculative fiction, for the other, poetry.

Our goal? To disrupt our writing practice by snatching in foreignness, seizing the uncanny in all its strangeness.

But why?

Though it may be true that, as writers, we think we inhabit language, there are times when we feel language is not ours. And, of course, it is not. How exhilarating, we thought, to expand our horizons! And so, like two lovers in a provocation game, teasing and pulling while thrumming antiphons in a pulse of jouissance, much playfulness in the enfold of intensity, we chased after the impossible nonrule of emancipated association in reacting to each other.

We hope that in reading these prose poems you will make your own connections and draw, if you wish, your own conclusions and associations without working too hard, without trying to detect patterns or contexts that might decipher the covert intentions of uncapturable text. There is nothing homocentric to find here, no preferred way of reading that is key to opening some academic or other discourse. Touch the text, taste it, feel it—do not try to contain its abstract language.

We invite you to be part of a spontaneous conversation that comes along with no headings of love or childhood or death or dissolution . . . Each prose and its response is an echo or a divergence of an element that one author's text stirred in the other.

As award-winning poet and academic Prof. Oz Hardwick said in a radio interview with East Leeds FM, prose poetry trusts its own momentum—the rules of verse do not dictate it. Prose poetry is not for people who are afraid of language. It's start, off you go—musicality in the verse.

One might describe some pieces as complex, relentless, but above all, speculating or crossing borders in the fantastic playground of language. We invite you to leap onto the stage of your own imaginings, plunge into what Henry James called the house of fiction.

This is how we envision ours:

A single detached house tossed out of Speculate settles across your dreams. Skin, paper-thin, desiccated and scripted like a collage, covers the absence of doors, thresholds, verandas, stairways and footpaths. But there are windows and louvers that look out to rain-licked grasslands. This is a house unsealed, with the sky art and earth art washed or rolled into each other on adjacent floors and walls. The roof, unlettered, is made of two sliding suns of creamed panels, foundation-like. Round the back is a rope ladder that will win you over. Up, up you go. Enter with care as you would any fiction that blurs the boundaries of genre, mode or form, that goes beyond the written and borrows from the unwritten. Together we can interweave art with language and watch it shape itself anew in an endless process of spontaneity and play because we can be here and there and away, all at once.

It is our hope that perhaps you may allow *Speculate* to be interactive, that you may find your own deep pleasure in engaging with speculative dialogue and playing with fluid text unencumbered by logic.

Part I

Eugen Bacon & Dominique Hecq

[Hecq's italicized responses to Bacon's prose poetry]

Evridiki

Friends are not important—like plagues, they come and go, even blood is not thicker. But fate is another matter. Some fool in autumn had a drink in the dark, sought a taste of heaven in a street named Bagh Nakh. Found it in the hands of a runaway who raised a hand and plunged a dagger that clung to the idiot's heart.

You were born in autumn and so, naturally, hate spring. The scent of blackwood showering pollen. The air licked with gold where the buzzing of the bees deepens. The sudden opacity of it all. You run. Run away. Away from the visible and from the invisible. With the pollen clinging to your skin, the sun striking and the darkness beneath your feet settling, you are a living phobia. A fear of no consequence. Yet as eons pass in one beat of the heart, you hear the rustle under the trees. Taste the bite of death.

She steals at dawn

to a place of memory, a beloved place she can enter her stories. The way her fingers pad on the keyboard. The rush that sweeps through her body arrives her at an intersection where mind and fingertip are one. She needs practice sleeping in a little, her lover's breath heartfelt on her earlobe. But she runs when she can, to a play-filled memory enriched with mannequins she can chase, surreal encounters on red rock bicycles, oh, how she soars.

She feels adrift, like an autumn moth flapping its dusty wings until it rests on your windowpane on the far side of the world. Says there is no rhyme nor reason nor even any explanation for being. Sky pied, almost as perfect as the horse she used to ride. As for turbulence, the sky is cloudless; the writing not exactly cloudy, but cloud-gathering. Now it's raining streams of light on red rock bicycles.

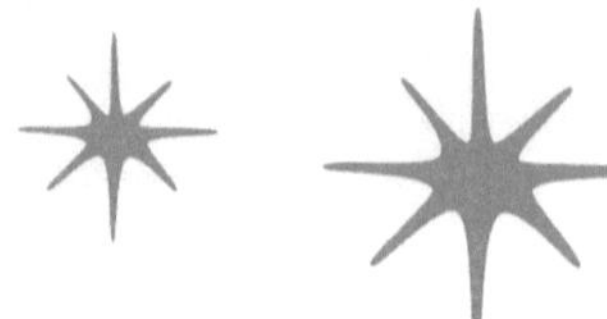

Let it play out

She wonders at the misjudgment of facts, the hybrid of the unknowing and the uncanny. Looking at the artist and his painting of the death mask, there is notable difference between a brief and a summons. In, out, who commissioned the sketch and to what detail of artwork? Out, in, beyond interrogating the plastic cast disunited from the corpse, how to discern confidence in an artist's perception? The plan is to keep silent, let it canvas out. Or perhaps to issue a bordering statement that is a responsible thing, or to conclude it's an illustration that is simply a hoax.

It is a hoax. All art is. We deceive ourselves, sometimes all the better to tell the truth, but deep down we fabulate, fabricate, counterfeit—lie about our deepest desires. As should be. I've just picked figs from the tree and painted them, knowing full well it's plagiarism in the history of art. Now I'm going to stew them, French style: Flambé Figs. Peel them carefully (12 of them). Put them in a heavy-based frying pan. Add 3 tablespoons of curaçao and the same amount of brandy. Sauté them over low heat until the figs take on the color of the painting. Prick them gently. Set them alight and shake the pan until your flame dies. Serve them warm with whipped cream. Sprinkle them with hoax dream powder. Enjoy!

Overrated

She returns home each day, ten hours in the office. She steps through the door, man, he's got the look. It's like *Here doggy!*, tail going wag, waiting for a ball. Just the gleam in his eyes . . . Work's so hard, bitches everywhere, she says. Let me love you until you feel right, he croons. He steals candles, makes her promises. Pricks her fingers, sucks her blood. It's a balance of costs, risks and benefits.

Returning to Australia after four weeks in Europe is a shock. It's not just that everything looks rougher, brighter, wilder, harsher in the morning light. No. Scary dreams overflow the days. I ride a Harley on the Monash Highway. Climb Mount Kosciuszko. Build space shuttles complete with orbiter, external tanks and solid-rocket boosters. Repair cassette tape recorders and telephones with curly handset cords. I steal candle snuffers, make wax candles and tallow tapers that are supposed to be dripless. But are not. I knock down burners, tip over charred candle wicks, snuff, snot. Prick my fingers on the candlestick's pricket. Dream of devotionals, the obliteration of the word phobia, and coins on my eyes.

Outward declarations of inner decisions

Today's word is jazz. You can hear her nimble feet gyrating in your head to no effed-up beat. She leaps and twirls to a place of memory, but it is full of compost and she regrets nothing. The motionless CCTV monitor captures her arms and feet as they pirouette in and out of the gaze's focus. The world keeps turning. Frolicking grounds full of water gardens connect the nerves that travel through the body, as balloons with eyes go *sway, sway* to the pitapat, rat-a-tat, pitter-patter pat . . . The sound is a love offering. She only wants to conquer herself in a trail of plummeting sand and too much poetry burning into a bard's cross-genre lyrics jousting with thought.

Rain burning the idea of love. The moon weathers the heart in haloes that tell of life unlived as though it knows desires given up for dead. It spooks me as I put the rubbish out, all the while focusing on promises we know we can't keep. Look! The moon exfoliates its light skin. Turns blue, blood, black. And now you will ask yourself why the chambers of your heart are patched, not lined, as if some invisible hand had undertaken to paint the pain over before it could be ciphered, named, encrypted. And you do ask yourself as you throw artichoke leaves into the compost, and run inside to the sound of jazz.

Neither a kitchen nor a sky

Her heart is a room full of photographs and pillows wafting around rehearsing melancholy and reinstating torment. But there is still no word, just somber silence in the floating photographs and neglected pillows cartwheeling like burnt toast past the IKEA blender and microwave in a fairy tale of space that does not involve breathing.

His heart smells of burnt toast. If you look closely, you will see a paisley design—the sort found as all-over design for an IKEA bedspread. The main motif and the background of ferns are done with pure (that is unmixed) colors: just red (turkey) and black (jet) to conjure up the marriage of blood and vegemite, the staples of his diet, as well as his sign in the Chinese horoscope. Yes: he is a tiger. Enter the chambers of his heart at your peril. Don't say you were not warned. He grinds his teeth.

The traveler

Her heart is a free tram zone, pedestrian crossings, traffic lights, wheelchair access, all hand-drawn. It's a labeled platform full of ads by a twaddle of writers saying glance at this, glance at that, and oh look! Free Wi-Fi. DO NOT OBSTRUCT. It's the yellow and black caution for passengers about a station upgrade, valid tickets, feet on seats, offensive language and taking rubbish with you. If there were words, she would follow the golden line at the platform, speak to it as the train pulled in. She would ask why she's not experiencing metamorphosis, just optical illusions about power operating doors gliding open and then shut, the train now departing. As she moves up the escalator past the cop shop with its blue and white squares all dirty as bootlegs, no help at a glance, she finds the subway, and then a great big owl fully concrete in the landscape, directing its gaze at the flat crowns of metropolis high-rises that defy or define the city. Like an authorized officer she knows that she must adopt a role that makes sure anyone with access to her toppled heart, delicate but still beating, pays their way. She walks past a teen sat cross-legged on the pavement with a ring on her lip and holding up a sign that says homeless, hungry and three months pregnant, but she keeps walking lest her heart staggers and stops.

Hey, you! You could be me. Life does go upanddown upanddown upanddown. This is why I dust the streets in your city, uncrease your creeks, polish your floors and occasionally collect your dog's droppings. I know there'll be spilled wine, broken glass, words curling from the fire in your mouth. A shudder. A pause. A da capo. I know that all too well. I peer through your window, and the pane reflects my shape making for the open road where our shoulders retain the weight of expectancy. Don't underestimate the virtues of polishing, especially in the Loire Valley where vineyards are doing well in the global village. There I looked after body armor adorned with intricate inlays. I preserved plumes and strengthened holders. I wiped visors, scrubbed chin pieces and gorgets. Straightened cuirasses. I polished breastplates and lance guards and backplates and codpieces and gauntlets and fan plates. And much more, my dear, as the word fan intimates. My nickname was chain mail, then chain fume. Try shackling me now.

From the lookout

The town is a bit of a has-been, any explorer can see from the wreckage of street signs and broken parks as you approach it. One fraying post says Pigs on a Boat, its arrow a crooked north, as another sighs windward and exposes a torn woman and remnants of what was once a domestication warning to roving fingers: Ten seconds on the hips, ten years—and then some—of a ring and much lip. A blistering sand guides away from dilapidation, from the pulled down town and broken job center, and races all the way into the sea where an adolescent siren draped in tidewash awaits to lure strays with her luminescent tail and fragmented song.

It's all a has been. A symphony of cloud puffs across the sky like the spirits of children failing to climb the chain of dreams rising higher and higher than the moon disrobing large and yellow among wing-beating shadows, its stilled tongue tied to forests, waterfalls and chariot-charged winter. Lies we tell until we hear gods laughing so hard the universe splits its sides and music falls from the stars.

A wail of sirens

It's late morning and dusk is drawing nearer, rushing up your personal preference for the man on the radio hammering nails a hundred ways at the stroke of midnight. In the valley of sirens, all dirges uncertain, they exploit the dark and wail *rrrr rrr* through the night. Playlists just for you pound into blocks filled with rage, bash around a bit longer but you try and put the question rolled up in a ditty unaffected by the impotence of language or holes on Light FM. It's the rules.

♦ ♦ ♦ ♦ ♦ ♦ ♦ ♦

The power has gone off: one of these spectacular electric storms. I watch them roll in from the bay toward us in dramatic Goya swirls of charcoal as though swept by giant brooms. I wait for the spear of lightning that will split the sky. The roar of thunder that will jump me out of my skin and rock the house like a boat tugging at its moorings. I run around, shutting all windows. Having given up on ABC FM, you are oblivious to all this. Attack me with pleasure in your dreams. Rrrr. Rrrr. Rrrr. If it were not for the impotence of language, I would say this is a gentle chainsaw massacre. I light a candle. Pour a glass of Pinot. Enjoy the movement of the hand across the page.

Safest method

On close consideration, you would expect that much clout from a four-gallon throat. It seemed silly to be emotional from 8:30 onward upon discovery of the creature in the islands of Sirenum scopuli. One swat of her tail could beach a man's legs but it was her music! It shipwrecked men's hearts. I never imagined that you too would be enchanted. Your lust deserted our arrangement and I was close to starvation in a drought so fibrous, I gnawed for hours on the bald bones of affection. Fruits and flowers are the only food, cooed the mermaid with her entrancing song. Torn between hunger and want, a desperate longing for touch, I traveled over a thousand miles. When I got to the moonlight, you were secretly shadowing my mirage, but I discovered a tonne of rage instead of a billabong. Time is up, let them eat dust, chorused the enchantress in the depths of your core, even as I dragged you through the labyrinth and chewed on your broad back, vultured on your biceps.

Was it the music that shipwrecked men's hearts? Or was it the voices? Using the shortcut of philosophy, I want to unshadow your mirage. You might hate me for it, but it's for your own good. Remember how Plutarch tells the story of a man who plucked a nightingale and, outraged at finding little to eat, cried out: You are just a voice and nothing more? So it is with your siren's song of fascination. From Homer to Derrida it has been an enduring erotic and philosophical concern. The siren's voice made men mad with desire, silencing the voice of their conscience. When time is up, Eros exits and Thanatos steps in. Now let me spread a banquet of flowers and fruit and nuts at your feet. I'll feed you grapes and pomegranates, nasturtiums and rose petals, sugar plums and cherries, cornflower filaments and artichokes plucked from the firmament. Don't worry about the pips. I know how to turn them into shooting stars.

Tugging at the waves

The water is a world of luxury, paradise where dolphins and otters rebuild their lives and sharks have leverage to moderate the price of loyalty. A million barrels a day for a few more dentists specialized in shark tooth, the sound of their plaque and calculus scrapers, the blink of their probes and operative burs differentiated from whale song in an ecological crisis. The new wave of dentist migrants on skilled visas puts a siege on the ocean in this new war that is also an existential crisis, and shoals of fish float face up, adrift along the edge of the shoreline. There is no radio.

Meanwhile the old wave of psychiatrists compounds the siege on the ocean in the war that is also the earth's existential crisis. Shoals of fish float face up, adrift in rivers and along the edge of the shoreline, high on deadly anti-depressants, eyes riveted on the evening star, forgetful to the fact that Venus is not a star, but a planet moving on an orbit closer to the sun than us and so always in close proximity to its shimmering being, whether it is rising in the east, or sinking in the west as we sizzle and soon crackle and pop.

Saving the Great Barrier Reef

Get out of the way, you bloody carcass, cries the unnamed scientist in the photograph. She is holding a chainsaw in a race to rescue the reef. The *burrrr* of the saw scatters a bunch of sunset gazers in a peaceful gathering and the scientist blows them an IOU. No matter how glorious the night, she roars, a morning is coming. She takes the leap and swims from one coral to the other, scaling off brown slime and ashed calcites to resuscitate the dead coral. But, faced with prospects of speeding up regeneration, the chainsaw splutters and malfunctions, leaves the marine biologist wondering if her purpose is to become a sea simulator in a world of evolution. She gulps gallons of salt water and falls back gasping. Waterlogged, she sighs. Little colonies of sea pens, anthipathes, staghorns and blue coral sprout in fluorescence from her mouth and ears. The urgency of her solution is real, but the environmental group strikes against this type of harvesting, reef in a human body. Someone captions the photograph: *Skeleton*

Once a rescue dream, the Great Barrier Reef now lies between us. Let's drop the pretense: we have become strangers. Even to ourselves, now that the plot thins and sentences molt and words fly toward the total immargination of language. The first word to vanish was truth. Do you remember how we quarreled like fowl in the wild, clawing at the air on the spur of the moment, beating our breasts? How mother's small teeth arranged themselves in a grin one Christmas over a dry turkey as she said our most edible parts would have to be our heart, liver, gizzard and giblets? How we laughed. And kept laughing as chicks and poults and capons dropped from her lexicon to the day she craned her neck and her breath died in a high-pitched note. I swear it was an A.

The wing of silence

In the emergency of the fish kill report where a cyclone brought gale-force winds and a rip caught three surfers enjoying the sea swells, it was not the cyclone or the rip that killed the fish, and not even the surfers who did the murder. Just the bruised shopping wraps from the nearby arcade and their colors of rainbow and frost, that's what. Just the disused bottles from the gentleman's club, all snapped into bags and dumped ashore with their crown corks and flip tops and screw caps but none worse than the plastisol and foamed polyethylene caps, that's what. The beach closed before noon, with more warnings of danger along the side—not a result of monster tides that gobbled topless teens who never follow any procedures but crumble under pressure. It was the result of erosion that emerged from checklists and IOUs striding inland from imagined cities between here and there, and they were beautiful, so beautiful, you didn't notice, oh, so blind.

The beach closed before noon as the atmosphere heated and expanded and the reef dissolved and ran. The waves died on the broken wing of silence. A loud bang. It all went black. A giant star shot up where the sapphire sky used to be, exploded and froze. Spun. Fell in a black hole named Whiting. Like a fish out of water, it sprouted gills twinkling with finger-like filaments, grew rainbow fins and a mouth that gulped in the dark. Crystals formed and arranged themselves into a villanelle.

None of this is a dream

Mars is an ocean and a beach, giant and mysterious outside her door. She imagines over and over the thrill, the exhilaration of sprinting on yellow sand as it burns, swimming naked against giant blue waves as they whip her face, scooting up a green and black pylon and it hugs her nakedness, releasing the rope under a fierce scorching sun and slapping feet first into the ocean as it roars.

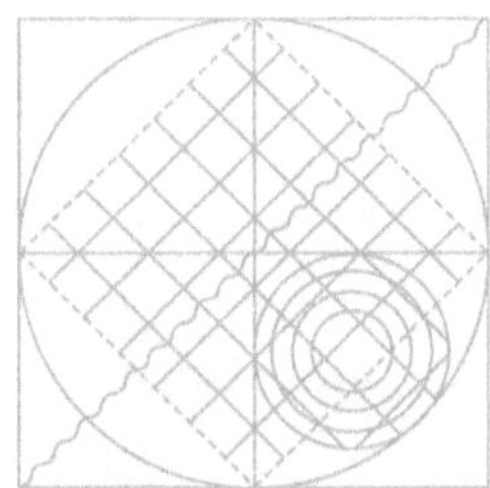

I'm glad I'm not C.G. Jung. I would bundle your dream in a textbook. Don't be afeared, I'm a benign Martian. I don't dream. Just move on. Most often than not I mimic realists and their pop art approach to living. Though I have a lot to say about piles, pylons and pythons, I focus on the detritus of consumer society. This I achieved after reading a Marxist PhD by a fellow called Strange, which repurposed my own experimental mosaics, collages and assemblages. I'm now considering a mural in exchange for conversation with humans. If that sounds too esoteric, the time may come when public art becomes more relevant, and therefore less estranging, through uncanny circumstances.

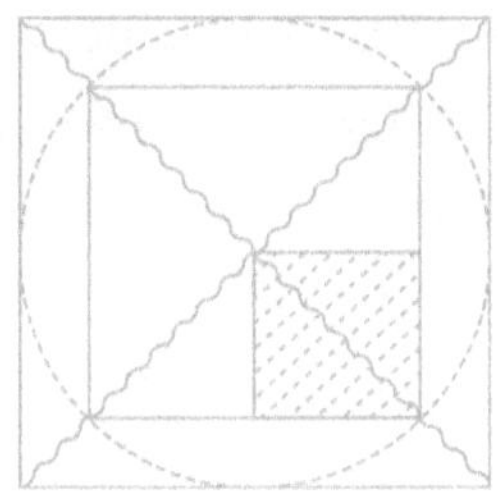

What the window saw

The wide-open window was astonished at the opportunity to unhinge herself and go see the world. Open and still open, she soared away from the timber cottage, over the trees and far away. Somewhere between a hillock and a river, and it was a day and a night, perhaps more, she saw a church in the center of a void and figured it was Sunday. The preacher was a penguin, the choir an assortment of sparrows and gulls. The drummer—a dugong or a sea cow—was using his forked tail and flippers to clash the cymbals, and in between percussions made a chirping and barking noise that made everyone feel like mating. Alerted by the sparrows' chattering and sharp notes and the seagulls' *ha-ha-ha-ha* and *keow* song, the faithful fell apart to see the shadow that had appeared and now stood silent at the pulpit. Who was to know that, in between mating and the need to kneel and pray, the creative pastor's rogue app update spiked with heatwave would slot in a visit from the prime minister to the church that day, and he was there to discourage the debauchery? The window added this revision history to her Tweet and was happy to rehinge back at her natural posting in the timber cottage, where she stayed open, still open.

As a window of a mature age, I can vouch for the fact that light and sight (including sight-seeing) are overrated. In the history of windows, there are three periods to be reconsidered: those of transparency origin, those of modernist tendencies, and those struggling to crystallize an identity in postmodern postcolonial times. Established windows, rather than dedication to transparency or, later, translucence (as was the case in plain pane times), tend to favor opacity in order to record experiences that are relevant to the lives of those who fail to clean them. Under the patriarchal authority in a postcolonial nation, emergent windows dream of going underground to capture the shades of what they see as unhinged, trivial, marginal, smeared and distorted.

The bird woman

travels the countryside to find time and contemplate the myths of a brand-new body whistled in song, plucked in a ukulele that vibrates with the wind. Mistakes in the everyday enable the music and its nettles of sound blanched in sky water. The bird woman swoops down to rekindle memory.

After she flew too close to the sun she had an MRI. Small amount of radioactive material. She was surprised to see the nurse would not administer it but wheeled her out a machine the size of a microwave. Said: come hither my ride fractionator. The nurse didn't blink. She programmed how much stuff was to be used via a screen and then stuck a needle into the bird woman's arm. And oh, mirabile dictu, *the liquid was dispensed the minute she pressed the red button. A smooth, cold ride. Machine love.*

A fair treatment

The sudden-death touch down inspired by exploits of the fabled Ma'a Nonu stoked fears in the American and Canadian squirrels and became a potential moment of sectarian violence. Rather than tackle the rest of the field, the black squirrels began to fight with the fox squirrels and both turned on the Aussie squirrel who refused to lash back—torn on matters of identity: why, oh why, didn't anyone deem him a native possum? He simply squeaked and barked, dodged claws and pads. The Eurasian pygmy shrew that was also the referee became the source of escalation with the loss of her temper when nobody could understand her *chit* and she took to her teeth. It was the Russian otter, a mere assistant ref, who found a way around the situation, soaking up half a bottle of Napoleon 1875. Imported. And though his act iced the on-field brawl, the Rugby Association—mostly French marmots, all elite—interrogated him fifty hours straight, and determined much evidence of collusion.

Death is trendy, not a collusion. It feasts on the tongue of the elite, journalists, and posthumanist commentators. It features in our prime minister's speeches, newspapers, literary magazines, anthologies, cartoons, zines and on websites. I heard death ooze out of a rap song like curdling blood as I approached the western wall of parliament where graffiti was being erased—something to do with deaths in custody. We don't like to hear about that. Say it's gravely exaggerated. The sudden death of children is subjected to the same kind of erasure—except when they die at sea on a boat that capsized: then it's sensational and outrageous; almost pornographic. When my husband, a pathologist, talks about the sudden and unexpected death of our child, it is matter of fact. It concerns itself with graphs. There is no shame. No grief. But over two millennia, women have spoken of pain, shame, blame, plotting against male discourse. They have spoken the unspeakable, unpresentable, unimaginable.

Green water, emerald sky

A child climbs to its feet the first time, falls, totters, falls, totters again, keeps at it a day or two, mirrors instinct, pictures success. Doesn't go, it's the finer detail, treading's not for me. Doesn't unlearn the falls, never studies impact. Just disremembers it's a manana, until it finds a banana and gathers speed into a wobbly waddly gone amble, lope and gallop into green water, emerald sky. You decided you would chant a dirge for humanity at your birth, chuckled as we snipped your umbilical cord. When you wrote a letter to the Pope asking that he crucifies himself for the sins of the church, I understood your vocation as a concierge. To watch the world ignite itself, and sing as it burns.

In the broken bones and middens of our emerald sky, the shrink and I work the sand of memories. With our spades, we build mountains and castles and towers. We hollow out tunnels and dig riverbeds. We bury our bottoms, feet and legs on the littoral, erasing all traces of the Middle Ages—fortresses, battlefields and armies—the War of the Roses, Blue Beard, Eleanor of Aquitaine, Vasco De Gama, Christopher Columbus. The First Fleet. The Suffragettes. The Great Eclipse of the Aboriginal Sun. We uncover chocolate wrappings, chewing-gums, hairpins, toothpicks, knife blades, nails and screws. Shells, ammonites, plastic pearls. I unearth a shattered honeypot, a Spode plate. The arm of a doll. A bottle top, dead match. A bird's thorax with bones like a miniature harp. I try reviving the dead bird. Sing Ten Thousand Miles Away!

Skipping across reeds and bricks

Like a child there is no danger field, no price checker. Nothing is poison, worry or toil, everything is food, sleep or play. Here come the Teletubbies, dance with the Teletubbies. There's room for today, always today, never tomorrow. Pajamas rainbowed with life's circus jazzed with the belly laughter of red-nosed clowns waltzing tippy-toed with the tigers one act away from the trick ponies. Skippy all carefree, many cuts, still no scars. Come rain, come shine, still no study of the weather because like a child you carry sand to castle where you want to be.

Crouched at the mouth of the river, the children catch eels, their fingers hooked in the sludge that will suddenly come alive with licorice limbs soaked in light, seasoned with sea. They never keep them, the eels. Nor do they attempt to hold back the sea, bright in the setting sun. Pangs of hunger will push their feet ashore, and they will skitter up the path, their tongues thick with the taste of salt. And home.

She often called on her

. . . during the little girl's chores into the night. Not only to
hearten her but to pass on the calming in her breath. The
child was grateful, but uninclined to respond as she hand-
washed the library floor in its marbled serenity in the foster
home. It was midnight and a sweet aroma of baking, warm
honey and cinnamon, wafted from the kitchen below—or
was it from the spirit godmother with her white tunic and
nurse's cape? Her own mother had somehow lost her. Later,
the child would read by torchlight, as the godmother danced,
a riot getting closer.

Once, the child sat by the opening of that labyrinthine library between a dark angel and his gossamer-clad acolyte. She pointed her boat out to sea, clutching memories of life and love, only to return to the shore. Its slippery pebbles, white and porous, soon gray with soot and red with rust: these bled in trails of flickering flames. Borges's hair was on fire. He said poets must remain with the concrete image because all language is abstract. The child nodded. Borges smiled. Said all we can ever work with is the experience of five senses. The child replied there are more than five senses.

Blood and sweat

The kitchen is alive with old knowledge. Red dust, oregano leaves, cockerel feathers. Dried flowers adulterate dainty cucumber sandwiches garnished with pickled shallots, arrayed on an edible cake tray. Her labor pangs strike as she is arranging warmed plates and polished cutlery on the table. On crooked knees she sinks. The baby oozes out like brain matter and opens its maw. "Dear mummy, just so ravenous."

As though at the center of some unspeakable spectacle, the mother opened her mouth. No sound came from her throat. Hers was knotted with the omnitemporality of women's guilt. She would need a double axe to cut through the knot. If only she could wake to her senses, she thought as she noticed a golden eye at the center of a spider's web in the corner of the kitchen window. A knock at the door. She looked at her progeny. Gripped herself tight. The golden orb opened its mouth. Said I'm going to gobble you up.

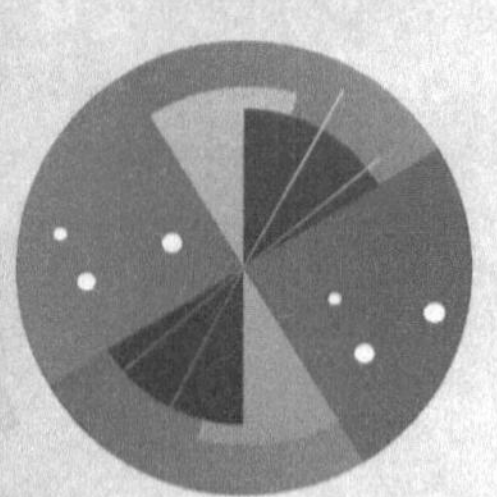

Choices

What your daughter did was kiss the devil boy who wore russet curls and the tattoo of a serpent around his neck. And when it was twilight, bang! shouted the door. Jesus, cried your partner Val, unclothed from the bed. A snatch of rifle from the chiffonier, at once with the snap of wood and a tumble of door off the hinge. Ruby eyes, saber teeth and the yawn of a black-bellied snake dove into your room. A roar swallowed the bullet, and a she-beast cuffed Val across the room . . . Then it was just you. In your trembling hands, the book of gods. What were you? But the ruby dimmed, and your daughter's eyes drew inward. The charcoal serpent recoiled into a tongue, the beast in the saber-tooth fled. And all that was left was you and a choice to sit it out, or belly dance until dawn.

True. I danced until dawn. We were hungry. Been hunting for kina roe all afternoon. A restaurant with kina on the menu might have served exotic fare, but it was closed. Even the markets sold fakes: if it's the real thing every stall displays the stuff on silver platters adorned with labels featuring KINA in gold letters (price undisclosed). All the little orange tongues of New Zealand may be delicious, but kina roe is way above excellence. That is the only thing we agreed upon. I've tried a number of imitations. Flavorsome, though lacking that je ne sais quoi *you find in Keri Hulme's* The Bone People. *I might head downtown, try the Rocks. Leave through them, and find my daughter whose eyes drew inward.*

Beware

The exiting vehicle took me on the cusp of no different. It all happened in a wink, interrupting the clean road that denied wrongdoing. But the evidence in my vision told me of a collision and there was the skin, the largest organ on the human body, all flat in place of tarmac. Dragon spots on the curb, it was 40 degrees Celsius, 104 degrees Fahrenheit, led to charcoal toes of the victim who responded that grass may be greener, just not on the other side.

An exiting vehicle not only trimmed my line of vision, it brutally interrupted my life. I was off in a cloud of smoke generated by the latest bushfire, not the exhaust of my Volkswagen UP! on my way to replace a faulty frontal Takata airbag when a semi-trailer hit me sideways. It was 36 degrees Celsius, 96.8 degrees Fahrenheit. The force of the collision caused the faulty airbag to go off with such exploding force that sharp metal fragments shot out and ruptured the airbag inflator. My lungs burst. Heart stopped. Brain scribbled away on the emergency screen until you turned off the machine.

It's a beatitude

Blessed are they with an endless fascination for fresh turmeric, for they shall receive a floral fragrance that stains yellow, oh, such levels of escapism. Blessed are they who sum up life where no one ingredient is complete on its own, for even flour needs milk or eggs or yeast to make it whole. Add ground ginger, black pepper—boiled and strained—honey and lime and good night spells in two ways. There's a bed with no sheets or pillows, no place to rest, someplace to cry. An ivory ceiling with the memory of you. I listen to the sound of our disconnect: maybe it's rugby or cricket, for sure it is not tennis—not ocher enough for you. The TV roars as I accumulate your lost scent and wait for your footfalls on the frayed carpet. Fair dinkum, blessed, am I?

Blessed are peanuts. For I've never been a finisher of fiction. I dig into dreams and surface into the bare realities of pantries and sour actualities of fridges. Today, I attend to the pantry. Attack packets of spices long gone dormant. Tarragon, cumin, cinnamon, cayenne pepper, paprika (mild, hot, smoked), herbes de provence, cardamom, basil, rosemary. Even the cloves have lost their scent. Out they go. On the lower shelf, I notice a row of vials filled with fresh chili, garlic, oregano, ginger, vanilla, sage, black pepper and turmeric. Sit at the table and allow the light to enter, not by accumulation, but accretion of figurative gestures. Consider the grain of the wood. Find those two peanuts you left when you raided the pantry for anything. Bless them.

It is sizzling

chicken thigh fillets on the hob. Pumpkin and pine nuts, cube size and ovals, carrot oranges and colors of cinnamon. Green beans and hock, a creamy risotto with pesto and blistered tomatoes. What's there not to like? He dashes out for thyme and parmesan, behind him the sound of an empty house filled with fat relief under a knowing moon, and when he returns only a thin thread guiding this fragmented love to sun-like stars. A chance last night for historic coupling as the clock struck twelve, the side of the bed he's not permitted to stay. Surely he knows this?

But his boner says no.

His boner says no. The sun came out at full height in the woods after that scrumptious meal. Go away, sun-like stars, you say. Take back your bloody superiority and secrecy. We like it dark here in the singing tree. Oh, don't worry. It's not about love, sex, death. Sheer pleasure is when we turn on our torchlights and spot invisible hands and grab the petals strewn on artificial grass pillows that cause lullabies to lull. In the undergrowth, intact buds. Silence. And then, a clatter of gutturals and sibilants collapsing unto the absence of breath.

On reflection he did not know

how to put thought into words, to ask why his tears were polished apples carved from basswood, full of caraway seeds that fell to his hips. They were tears so aromatic and imbued with an earthy taste of anise, but there was no precipitation. Just an acid base that was richly oxidized and reacted with her elements to generate heat, but so slowly she hardly noticed. Truth is, his tears unraveled something, incited events into motion. On the fringe on a myth, she tugged him past the lobby, up the lift as he cried. They fell into the fug of a room full of rustic walls and baby trees lined on the mantel, as he cried. Sheeny woodwork from his eyes rained on the floor, crescent-shaped seeds pounding her stockings and his shorts. Are your tears psychic or basal, she asked as they shared a cigar in the afterglow of lost rain. Feathery leaves like beards on a wall shook on the balcony of their hotel. He said, Sorry? And fell fast asleep.

No. He did not know how to push thought into words. And sorry was definitely the word he could not use, let alone utter. He heaved the bin against his hips and legs and hauled it to the front of the yard. He stood unmoved in the dark where the path becomes lawn. Truth is, the yard may have been forbidden ground at dark and the wall would have made of the night a high fence but for the light in your window where he knew you would take off. On the fringe of the dark, he leaned into a myth. Lines of melted wax fell from the sky. White light turned dark. He stood with aching shoulders, wished sensational headlights away as he did, earlier, headlines, and dismissed the idea of logging into cloud. He thought of sleep.

Random calls

on satisfaction rates resuscitated the remembrance of a service provider's last words on taking farmers into the future with high tech high performing gizmos, just months before sales collapsed, and it was personal and not measured, the fond farewell muffled by newer and brighter experiments, jets soaring from the ephemeral to unveil other modifiable risks that reminded me of my ex who was a dentist and a drummer. It is funny and sad. He drove an uber.

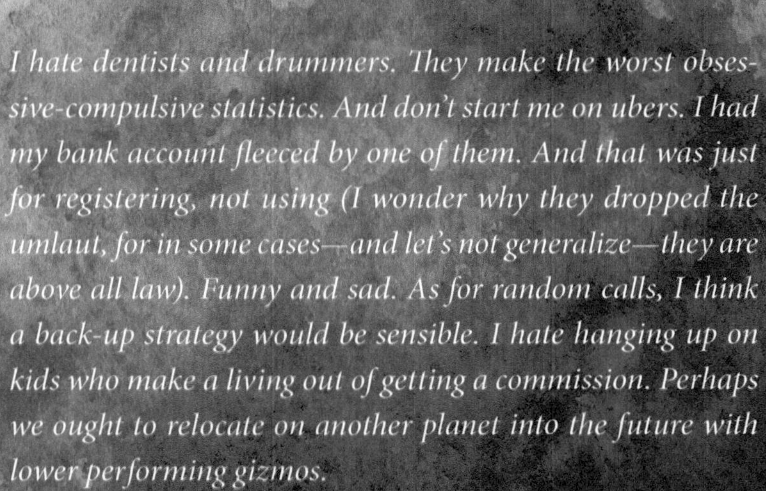

I hate dentists and drummers. They make the worst obses-
sive-compulsive statistics. And don't start me on ubers. I had
my bank account fleeced by one of them. And that was just
for registering, not using (I wonder why they dropped the
umlaut, for in some cases—and let's not generalize—they are
above all law). Funny and sad. As for random calls, I think
a back-up strategy would be sensible. I hate hanging up on
kids who make a living out of getting a commission. Perhaps
we ought to relocate on another planet into the future with
lower performing gizmos.

The man in my bed

Is a conversation with a shoe. Are you comfort or protection, fashion or necessity? You say you're a boot, full of grip and stability—great for all weather. I say you're not leather, for leather is breathable, it absorbs humidity, and what I feel is drowned. Then a pair of sneakers, you laugh, everyday wear, a great sport. But you break down easy, I say, and I'm growing bunions, so you can't be sneakers, no flexible sole there. Crocs that what, you say, cool right here, ready for the beach. But you're not light as a feather, I say. There's no walking on air and sometimes wedge heels or lace ups counter the past's frame and are uneasy to slip off. Then what? you say. Run, that's what. *Run!* urge my feet.

I run away! Run! Run! He says I need you. I need you. He was never a good kisser. Love-making hasty and always in the same missionary position to the sound of François Campion's "Courante la Victoire." No adjustments, viewpoints to counter that past's frame. I ought to wonder what went wrong, but look at the sky. There is an opening left of the moon. I am ready to tackle new options called matelot du ciel, *or let's just say sky sailor, as the main character.*

The man on the street

with a tawny head and a sleeve of tattoos, a big fella, he lives a voice activated life that speaks through his silence. The angle of his lean against the pillar at the bus stop, the nudge of his finger connecting transitions through his smart phone, the secret of his smile at a tweet or a gossip or a fact or a gizmo surrounds you with the noise of absence in scarlet pimpernel bloom. Speak, begs the garden of your soul as sand flows through the hourglass. Speak, weep your souls, too many of them now, for we are listening. And he says, "Ok Google, beatbox for me."

Beatbox: a drum machine, a radio or cassette player used to play loud music, especially rap (thanks, Google). I feel completely alienated. I am a techno-retard not at all partial to vocal percussion, especially if it involves the art of mimicking drum machines using your mouth, lips, tongue and voice. Nor am I interested in vocal imitation of turntablism, and other musical instruments. Too old for hip-hop and hipsters. Definitely not my kind of poetic vision. Come to think of it, if it could be danced . . .

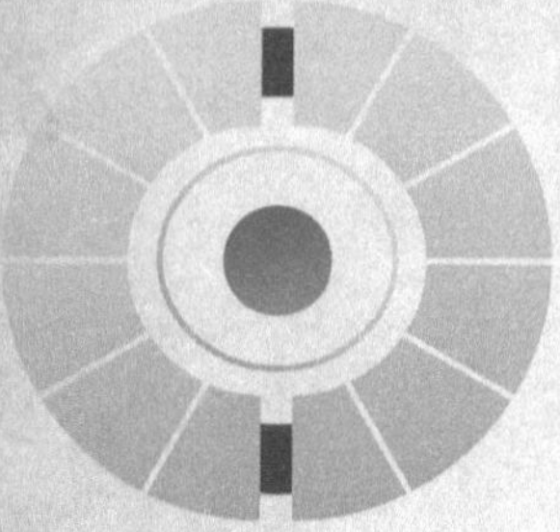

Surprising things he owns

A full-on bomb shelter in the left ventricle of his heart that encloses him from the nuclear explosions of anarchist women. A briefcase containing money, silver, watches and a dog-eared note that says: Save yourself. The portrait of an orange-tinted viper, white-lipped, making its debut at a royal tea party that marks the official birthday of a reigning monarch. A trapdoor to sanity across the river just beginning to turn emerald on whose floodplain he cooks naked but wears a flesh-colored apron within which he carefully tucks his three testicles.

A flesh-colored apron within which nothing is in working order. A pet magpie that sits on his shoulder and pecks at chunks of silence. Eyebrows like auto-reflexive question marks and eyes the color of amber when struck by sunlight. Long silver hair tied up in a tight knot at the back of his head. A PhD on flash fiction that discusses the form's unique ability to create energy and engagement through patterning and omission, compression and connotation, line tension and sound intensity. A postmodern library lined with books he calls dissipative systems of high creativity indivisible of the embodied minds that read them. A jumping time piece. Crypto money in the gaps.

Sorry for the false start, I suppose it's autumn

First thing each day my story begins with passive narration, like some distant documentary, both in first person and as a you-narrative. I lose him straight into an odorless sewer, no sign of decay or fusty smell, something, anything that could create methane and generate electricity that volts him up to curiosity that keeps us sweet. So he chooses to wade into platonic friendship and a connection that culminates in a blind date with the bestie's girl in a bar. But at this stage . . . the first person or you-narrator doesn't care. Six pages of it, or is it months or years, there's cruelty or revenge in the Samburu Reserve and, like an elephant, I raise a foot over his body and scatter his bones.

You were born in autumn and so, naturally, hate spring. The scent of blackwood showering pollen. The air licked with gold where the buzzing of the bees deepens. The sudden opacity of it all. You run. Run away. Away from the visible and from the invisible. With the pollen clinging to your skin, the sun striking and the darkness beneath your feet settling. You are a living phobia. A fear of no consequence. Yet as eons pass in one beat of the heart, you hear the rustle under the trees. Taste the bite of death.

Locating

One way is the pull of a rug from under your feet, and you don't see where to stand or go, there's just war with gravity in a cloud full of riverbeds right there in your living room. One way is giving up everything and he gives up nothing and there's no negotiation, just weeds of non-specifics and a common understanding that one of you is a loser. And it's not him. One way is the rumble of wind from his body in the dead of the night, half a gallon of air condensed into toots of excessive flatulence; as he turns in his sleep, you wonder what forever tastes like.

One way is a march in the dark where bullets scintillate like rough diamonds and cut through the air, your feet taking you higher and higher up a craggy path. One way is a ferret burrowing through the flesh of fifty thousand million years of volcanic activity. One way is the soft crest of a hill where you lose your balance and wage a war with gravity. One way is a river of clouds closing its mouth on the moon, dousing the stars and soaking the night. One way is a bolt of lightning searing earth and sky. One way is eternal return.

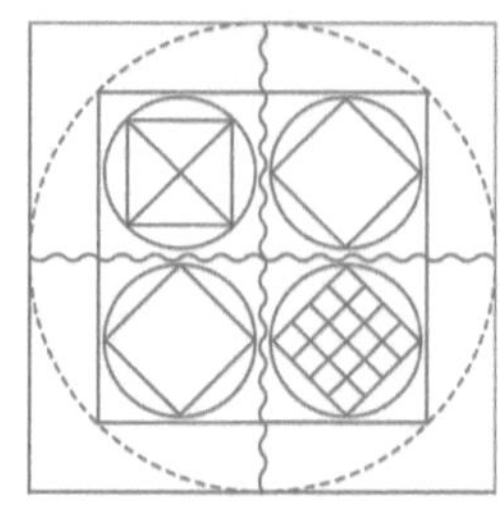

Life in monochrome

Inside a prison that is an eternity, politicians are husks shriveled to gnomes trapped in ancient skin so fragile it breaks and a gruel of insides leaks to the grimed floor, offering up a gift of dying in a penalty of undying. If you listen closely, you will hear a faint scratching of nails long as a Komodo dragon's on somber walls licked by a wash of tide and whispers from ashore in time after time after time inside the fossil tower on an island so unexpected, you are astonished anyone would go there. And if you work more characters into the story, you'll find an important writ both fascinating and disturbing in the profundity of faces wearing evil pressed to foreheads never too revolting to dissuade the photographer whose shutter clicks to stir the silence unwashed in dust, framed in a picture.

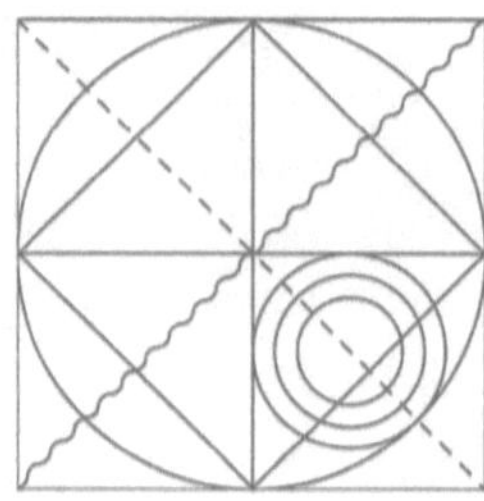

Life in monochrome is a sequence of events with limited pictorial potential and no chronology. It is a procession of scenes. Leading the procession are defunct gods playing silent music. Following them are dinosaurs and elephants, tigers and monkeys, cheetahs and pythons, crocodiles and meerkats, bison and camels surrounded by human clones and avatars from different continents riding bird vehicles or seated in their mock-celestial cars propelled by the desire to reach inland seas or lotus lakes where, lulled by the wind, flowers and bushes dance, sing or play music, swirling and twirling as though there is no dawn. The procession strikes a balance between hieratic dictates, chaos and uncommunicable cacophony. There is no dramatic impact.

Punctum

The history of silence is a stranger by your rib, and your togetherness is something physical that remains an abstract. The lacking comes along with the shock of realization, a whisper of something stolen but you can't put a shape to its value. Knowing in advance the types of nature versus nurture that no one will question speaks of eyes but no lips, scales inside a heart, not a wide brimmed hat full of hairpins. The system full of white silk and ribbons is compromised. But not obsolete in the punctum of flash fiction.

Some bodies can't be put to rest: the history of silence is a haystack. This one holds a hairpin I lost five decades ago playing dress ups. It belonged to my great aunt, a milliner and the spinster of the family. She'd say come any time dear. And sure enough I'd be at her modest house in Malines every holiday. It was dark there, but immaculate. In her spare room were two bags: one full of fabric off cuts and one containing a white silk dress, a pair of blue suede shoes with bobbin heels, a veil and two hats. There was a cream bonnet with ruching and frills and a ribbon bow. There was a brimmed woman's hat with stiff netting, smooth crown and indigo hatband from which a plume and a hat pin stuck out—my favorite. Picture me in white silk, high heels and veil. That's how I lost the hat pin that matched the clip that holds the tie to the unnamed man in the photograph my great aunt kept on her bedside table until her death. The punctum of a too short short story.

Hit and miss

It shouldn't come to this. Be still my pounding heart, it's the who cares cup, play on. Time to arrest history, you heard it on the radio. I was always awarding a freebie, letting you back into the game. Losing hours of my crumbling life, years—the orchestra still playing. There was never a deliberate rule, but it was sunny here, cold there, so I became a protector as I got on. Not really what you do, but I did, forgive me for drifting, for being out of touch, for awakening and knowing it's lightly contentious, like hugging a singing tree. Who did the hitting?

But we deserved the pain, right?

So the story goes. Bad, mad or sad, we were and remain Alices in Woundherland with big sad eyes straight out from a Blackman painting, pining for the moon. Just imagine doing the hitting. Counterpunch. Jab, cross, hook, uppercut, back-fist. Throw in a kick for good measure. I reckon we can show them our mettle, don't you? Oh, yeah. Turn into bleeders pretty quickly. Trouble is I can hear lawyers in the future of such a violent fantasy: We take this matter seriously and, as a consequence, are currently conducting our own internal investigation.

They will be deemed not to have deserved the pain.

Scorched

They sat in emphatic silence, navigating chopsticks, nibbles, tweets and texts, as they connected with the rest of the world but them. Their eyes met over stone fruit brûlé and she lifted the green dragonfly cast iron pot. "Tea?" she said, as though he were a stranger from someplace in history, and it was repeating itself. He looked at her as though she had just slapped him with a whole fish.

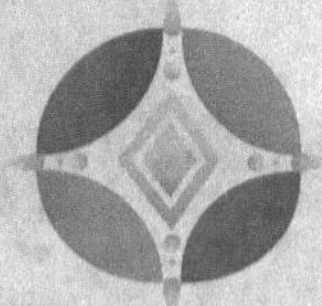

Ah! La jeunesse. Expecting the simple joys of gastronomy when menus and picturesque locations never compensate for mis-communication or desire. The latter often confused with sex. She should have slapped him with a whole fish of the groper species, just that tad tired with white enamel, not vitreous, eyes and pungent smell. Had there been an end to the meal, it would have been soufflé au fromage, usually an entrée. It could have been well-risen and golden brown on the top, if only the chef had been briefed to prepare it in advance. He would have known, as one does from years of practice, to halt the process after the egg yolks were added. He would have kept the mixture in a cool place and added the delicately whisked egg whites (soft peaks) just prior to baking in a perfectly preheated oven. Stone fruit brûlé may have been coveted. Granted. It was definitely the wrong choice. Brûlé(e) for burned, singed, scorched. You get the picture. As for stone . . .

Vestigial night

Mirror, mirror . . . we sip milk tea with unfinished pining, and what we murmur in the flowers circling the grapevine is not the greatest show of all time but the ramble of an earthquake that collapsed a tourist island. Out yonder in Southampton as a silver spoon dances in a golden broth, it floats to the surface white seeds that outline the end of a pen and the start of Hellboy and an evil sorceress sitting on marigolds. Mirror, mirror . . . a silhouette of M. Night Shyamalan whispers the story of a dark phoenix and thirty greyhounds, dragons and aliens in collision at an air force base in Vegas. How I bore you. A blue fly with overgrown ears races in shadow inside the pupils of a chef in a pop-up restaurant near a pet cemetery someplace in the whistle of our half-dazed sleep. What sort of affair are we going to see this time round?

What kind of affair? It's hard to tell. I'm a kinda down to earth bloke. Still stewing over a Union meeting where one of my mates got ridiculed. I can't remember what he said. Only just see him adjusting the straps of his overalls over his crumpled shirt and stooping to stuff his towel and plastic bags into his workbag. As he wiped himself and pulled the shirt over his chest he frowned as though I might have been telling the worst thing ever. I said he had not come out into the assembly as we all did, but tailed behind. I said he had not said a word as we all listened to the union report on his dealings with the managers and as he grew restless. Perhaps, I said, it seemed as though he had sought something to hold on to. The mirror was one-way as.

The bury ball

It was an era of the ballers, they bounced everything on showcase. First there was the money world, a financial circuit of coins rolling across screens and sofas. And then, in a NASA special, astronauts bounced along spherical planets, volley-balling spare oxygen in cylinders across the surface. But when the talk show came, with the greatest respect, parliamentarians uncloaked and flashed the live TV viewers and in an official statement declared an important difference in the art of war: *Don't make an issue out of it. All proceeds go to a non-profit charity.* This captivated the war heroes and they bounced nuclear ratings at the network. It prompted a redefined global excellence that involved optimism on a local level and it translated onto an international stage. This drew an apocalypse of intelligent aliens on extra-terrestrial visits only on circular nights, and they were not a danger to civilizations that did not argue or fight against them.

In that era when private lives appeared to be ruled by the force of historical events, people were contradictorily challenged by creative achievements that, even if originating in apocalyptic scenarios, developed a self-sustainable energy that superseded material circumstances and foreshadowed alternatives. No matter how intelligent the aliens, they were bound to be defeated by powerful artistic representations of how war and geopolitics create the plight of humanity. I must remember posting "An Earthling Sends a Postcard Home."

Unprecedented

The wandering cow like a serial bomber was desperate but defiant. She added daffodils and rainbows to each masterpiece and it traveled unchewed to the rumen and then to the reticulum. Satiated from the eating, she rested and waited and thought through stuff. She calculated the right time to cough up bits of cud, now chewing them completely before she swallowed. They raced through her gut, exploded from her bovine ass and splashed pat in a polychromatic mess on the polished shoe of a visiting president just checking in on his way to the next town with a new detail—most had mastered the perfect low ponytail, and those who hadn't wore tail-hair wigs. As cameras flashed, the cow took back to her eating and continued to be an artist ruminating to dung the next political dunderhead.

As cameras flashed, the cow took back to her eating and continued to be an artist ruminating on how to improve dyed patterned fabrics. She mastered the direct application process, the resist or indigo process, the mordany, madder, alizarian or modern process, the application of a thick pigment known as roghan made by mixing a yellow powdered color with castor oil and then heating the mixture. She perfected the art of representation and moved on to self-representation. I own a framed painted cloth that I keep in a safe where she figures with Sri Nathji, an incarnation of Krishna playing the flute and herself among a herd of fellow cows listening intently. The central figure, Nathji, is superbly executed in pichhavai Kishangarh style, coming alive in gold and encrusted with jewels. His neck and chest are draped in a profusion of necklaces and beads, seemingly defying the burdens of time, caste and geopolitics.

Nothing new

Life is a seagull walking barefoot on sand, connected to the soil. It's the greatest earthing. Look out across the choppy waves, kite surfers soaring on wind. The seagull hops from a whitewash, follows shoe prints on the beach that's so freaking cold, a blind man can see. Windswept: look at the tree shrub, see how it grows—aslant from the ocean. The seagull flaps its white wings, hops without settling on a vault bar of the beach gym. Hop, hop without stopping. Recover repeat. Yonder on the road, as darkness swells, cyclists branch to Danks Street, just before Nimmo Street. "Barefoot on earth," the gull says to no one. "The greatest earthing, so underrated. I had the biggest poop ever."

Life is a chameleon feeding on chance encounters subject to the whims of composite weather maps, or synoptic charts that display conditions over areas too broad to fathom where cold fronts and warm fronts collide, occasioning sudden changes in temperature and barometric pressure. Such maps don't have anything to do with cardinal points, let alone arrowheads, crossbars and feathers that seemed to give stability to the weathercocks adorning the churches, town halls and schools of my childhood. I hate the numbers around the station model. I always end up on a stationary front. Synaptic charts would be more useful. One could even imagine using a dual scale thermometer to record the fluctuations of human desire.

The nature of reflection

In a matter of blink and swallow, the piano riff thunders, sighs and drones to foreshadow a flicker of eyes in the oppressive dusk. Under interrogation it doesn't matter there's a super blood moon etched in the embers of the night. "Bring out those mugs," says the watcher. Three culprits shuffle slowly, slowly out of the holding room that is also a ghost of the 1885 Station Cafe. "These are not mugs, now there's a handsome rooster!" The culprit in question teems with life, *But I am a girl!* No one walks through her claim and they get down to probe the matter of fare evasion that landed the culprits in the conundrum of an interrogation that could go until six in the morning, then start over. You can collect side effects and a lifetime of ridicule where latitude doesn't help in accelerated focus on non-accountability oblivious to misinformation, uneducation or simply uncleverness.

Possible side effects unrelated to misinformation include at worst paranoia. At best, agoraphobia. I don't believe it. Truth came to stay when I was away. It's been six months (yes, it's been out to celebrate). Time to sum up developments on the theme of sharing space. It's noon and I'm in bed in a dark room keeping my mind busy in a kind of reversed situation. Nothing's happened except for the fact that Truth went through my cupboards and riffled through papers in the drawer of my desk where I keep my will, foreign currencies and Speculate manuscript. So furious was I that I looked up the web for flats to rent. Found one in Spacious City. Meanwhile, I found: a film titled "The Uninvited." It's giving me ideas for a different mode of reflection. Any bubbles of blood from your bite will be absorbed, not smudged, and I will play you Ravel's Bolero for good measure.

Part II

Dominique Hecq & Eugen Bacon

[Bacon's italicized responses to Hecq's prose poetry

History lesson

Again and again, the shrink and I work the sand on the beach in the backyard. Today, we build mountains and towers and castles in the air. We hollow out tunnels. Bury our bottoms, feet and legs in the squeaky sand, erasing all traces of the Dark Ages with its fortresses, battlefields and armies. In the blink of an eye gone are the Renaissance, the Restoration, the Discovery of the New World, the French Revolution, the Declaration of Human Rights. The Great Depression and the Return of the Repressed. We uncover broken records, heels, shells, husks, knife blades, pricks and spurs. Stirrups, crampons, hooks. I unearth a shattered honey pot, a bottle top, the head of a doll. Bones. I try reviving a dead bird. Look at the sky's vault. Sing (repeat) *Ten Thousand Miles Away*. I take a deep breath. A giant leap. Yes! I land on the moon and bump into Neil Armstrong.

Like a child in amniotic fluid, the violence that had plagued medieval mountains and castles hollowed itself underground through what was once a champion's tunnel but was now sim-ply a sewer, and hauled itself to the surface. It toddled across Flinders Street, found itself in a laneway full of coffee lovers and buskers no one wanted to hear. There, it took a breath and ignored an impulse to wail at the stares walking alongside its pockmarked fetal body. A legal studies unit encouraged thinkers to dissect this conundrum, as the biology lab would touch nothing of its saber teeth and hairpin bones wrapped in shells. But the leap came in fiction, a bestseller on the five senses of horror that livestreamed for decades and inspired a new documentary called Curtain Falls, its countless parodies including a cameo of the Pope and Madonna soaked in a bath-tub full of honey soaring to the moon without an arm strong.

Confession of a bookworm

The book is in a cardboard cover marked Fragile. I tenderly lift the volume out of its dogeared case. Scraps of leather binding and confettied paper fall on the floor in a cloud of organic matter. I wish I were an alchemist, botanist or physician, but my eyes naturally turn to calligraphy and flashes of color. I kneel. Sneeze. Finger the powder when out of the blue the Abbé Raynal storms into the library and screams: *malheureuse!* My fingers are red and as I try to rub the color off, the palms of my hands grow red. *Malheureuse! Dactylopius coccus* holds the secret of cochineal. You'll be tried for treason to the sound of Spanish, thundering cannons and French trumpets. You will receive angry salutes from twenty-four pounders. And you'll burn among phials and flasks and cases of books.

The book is in a quiet room, squeezed in a working space of strong opinions and no respect. Nothing reveals its abstract or a cover, no textual conditioning pointers or blurbs that will adulterate your approach to the text. No Unauthorized Entry, says the preface, but you lift the first page anyhow and discover the book is a lantern-lit building that acts with integrity and travels on a tramline. Pedestrians give way to it. As its doors groan and bang open you wish you were a song that is a child, so you could climb skipping and whistling into the lanterns and travel all the way to a dance of drowning souls.

Today's word is fire

You can smell it in the air. In full light, specks of ash twirl and swirl like a miniature beehive. The water is slick with sunlight. I dive in. Touch the bottom—unsettled silt, rocks, pebbles. Surfacing, I feel the water flowing ice-cold over my shoulders. I begin to swim. Long strokes upstream toward the fall. My chest expands, arms bracing the water. I don't feel the cold, but my toes and fingertips are numb. Dappled glare on the surface, then the brush of hair-like roots. I dive through the fall, water drumming my back. A red sandstone outcrop, porous soil, a cave. In one step, I'm inside. Wait for my eyes to get accustomed to the dark. On a slab of stone, a smatter of nuggets: reds, ochres, whites. On the walls, a splash of fingernail moons.

Today's word is donut, and it is butterflied, a clean split before a gobble. There are diners and waiters and chefs full of resourcefulness, but none equipped to tackle the donut as it leapt out of the dessert plate. Having endured the butter knife's cut, it was profusely wild in its escape attempt, betrayed by the pastry chef who had lovingly added yeast and self-rising flour, full cream milk and pure vanilla extract, watched it rise and golden. But the classic glaze, thin as a sigh, the cinnamon whiff that danced and dazzled, both meant nothing as the little girl dislocated the donut's top from its bottom with a blunt knife. Before she could drag it to her mouth, tear it with her teeth, the donut clapped itself shut and did a burn out across the table, landed onto a waitress's hands and she packed him into her pocket. The feel of her hands made him forget his destination, and he lay against her hips wound so tightly. The touch alone was enough.

Footnote

Ella knew she would not be able to make it to old age gracefully without a source of income other than earned from her pen and so she applied for a variety of jobs for which she received curt rejection slips, the latest being for the position of sandwich hand in a new age deli that specializes in dishes flavored by renowned international writers. An excellent cook versed in the history of gastronomy, gluttony and intemperance, Ella had thought her prospects were good. Sorry. No references, said the note.

The footnote took to questioning what might make a princess want to vanish, why a great poet was turning into a pump-kin, when a live TV host might resign with his dreams and violins, what a dead snorkeler was doing with a tired smile on a football field, and all such things that inspired sudden intellect. It was a matter of philosophy to find answers to these questions, to value knowledge and existence as much as reasoning and language. But the note found itself on a red carpet and everything that came from each celebrity's mouth disabled thinking. Distraught, the note surrendered to house arrest inside a room wallpapered with simple words and asso-ciations: able: fool / beauty: published / cruel: wet . . . you get the gist. Frustrated by the year, the note took to busking at Flinders Street Station, roaring emotive numbers of asylum seekers, nurses and first responders, and a few people hurled coins. To the note's astonishment, it won a Grammy.

Letter to a bride to be

Thank you for sharing with me the newest (yet quite retro) issue of *Vogue Bridal Patterns*. I love that off-white silk you brought back from your travels, it will suit your complexion perfectly. It looks much better than the Nora white organza and is a tribute to your integrity. I hope I'm not reading too much into your choice of color. Before you start making the dress, I urge you to indulge in an intertextual journey around your maiden room, if I may say so, for I'm not sure you know on what *galère* you are embarking. Mark my words. I don't mean gondola, or anything romantic, but galley, a low, flat ship with one or more sails (glad you opted for a visor instead of a veil) and up to three banks of oars worked by slaves. First, as an artist, you must re-read Tennyson's "The Lady of Shalott" against the grain. Then turn to Elizabeth Bishop's "The Gentleman of Shalott" and Jessica Anderson's *Tirra Lirra by the River*. I studied both in year twelve (wish I'd paid more attention). Finally, and this may surprise you, especially coming from me, read Henrik Ibsen's *A Doll House*, a work your father drew on to devise our home. I now think Ibsen understood the difference between need and desire; desire and love; love and lust. Your father would disagree, but I would maintain that Ibsen was really a proto-feminist writer. Wink. One last thing: beware of identifications. With two (anti)heroines bearing your Christian name, you wouldn't want to become unduly hystericized. Much love. X

In a letter to my silence, I study the keyboard for a space between sleepers and their dreams that may surprise you. Each dream is like sitting at the top of a house with no earthing, and it is right between power poles in the middle of side rain. Nothing is neutral, the dogs are howling at invisible warriors of the night. No one knows how it happens, but there's a breakout, and then tongues and tails. Wake me, my love. I need to hear the syllables of my thoughts. Xx

Lines

This line is lost in a science of nowhere, but somewhere is happening and it's growing through the night on its way to the moon. You are so beautiful, people stumble as you cruise. Trucks stagger at the crossroads, trams forget the lights have turned. A cyclist crumples in the gutter. You say, *Pardon?* This line is lost, asunder from the verselet, but you're so beautiful. The symmetry of nose to lip, the balance of your forehead, the array of hair on your head, dimples in your smile. Oh, what hue are your eyes? Classes suspended so teachers can gawk, pupils bundled to see through the casements, voices calmed but they fall infected, a drumbeat of rhetoric. What a wonderful view! Just a line, basic geometry, a lost line in the middle of a page, oh, so beautiful, you can fly.

This line has already migrated past the immargination of the page. It's moonstruck and I watch its metamorphosis with wicked fascination. We are made of letters, and letters both liberate and oppress. As I watch the text liquefy in the pool of light on the desk, thirst takes hold of me. Peel me an onion, I say. And you do. I am waiting for you to blink. For me to produce tears that will wash away all the lines and the words and the letters in the universe.

Ariadne dreams of a new relativity

Pitch black. No water. The monster's breath is cold and smells of carrion. Always in debt, once bankrupted, arrested and imprisoned. Now he's in hiding. Though he roars and curses and says the universe is but a huge expletive, I'm not scared (been there before). Shh. Shh, I say. Think of the metaphysical implications of black holes, dark matter, the big bang and string theory. We could expand the Labyrinth with a slew of metaphors. Slay all the fake gods of Logos, purge their purgatories, destroy limbo and generate new galaxies where you could hear the light. Touch sound. Wring the neck of death. Galaxies where shooting stars surge and rush, swell and sing to the glory of the Minotaur.

XOOOOX XOOOOX XOOOOX

*My mother slipped me a note and pushed me into a screen.
Pitch black. No water. And then lights. But the Minotaur was
hiding and slept all day, curled between the Americans and
some walking dead. When the cake boss roared and cursed,
and demanded chicken and waffles, a governor put black
holes, dark matter, on his face but forgot his pale hands.
People said it was part of the jump, a labyrinth. The time
team led by archaeologists to the big bang and string theory
in a windswept island off the coast of a new galaxy rendered
verdict that collided justice with reality. So I opened the note
and it said, Total Bella, and I wondered if it was vengeance, a
phenomenon or purgatory. I need a tip-line to the tattoo of us.*

Allegretto ma non troppo

You're an animal transmogrifying into a human after years of practice. A ritual starts with an early morning shave—the mirror, shaving kit on the shelf, razor, aerosol shaving cream. No after shave. At the basin, your head bows into lukewarm water. You wash your face with hot water from the tap and rich soap suds. Spray a handful of foam from the can, and with fingertips lather your throat carefully. Brush it over your chin, daub it over the upper lip. You lather your cheeks, and wonder why men talk to themselves at this point in movies. Leaning into the mirror, you steer the razor up and down your throat. Close. The razor nicks.

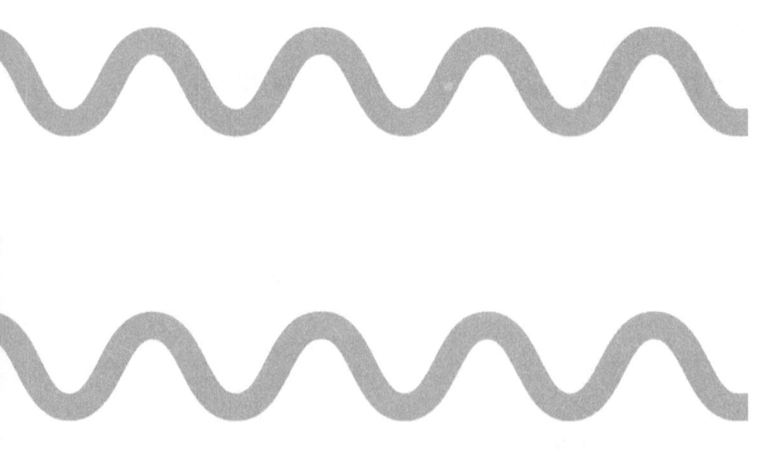

In times of deep suspicion, you put technology first in an age of the explorer despite swimming with big fish. Your ritual starts with witching for something in the parts of an ocean where the converging plates of lithosphere collide. Recurrent earthquakes lather you carefully with vibrations connected to a world of movies filled with sediment and underwater vent. The gases explode you to the front of a mirror that refuses to follow protocol and shows you in a light that's up and down and shocking, really—and she said?

Call me scar

Words tumble like clowns falling out of a hearse, and we're back to the old circus with all its lions and acrobats, says the wizard in the mirror, steeple-crown hat askew. I look like death warmed up. *Nuit blanche*. I ought to do my tax. My youngest turns eighteen today! Tick tock. Tick. Tock. Old people are supposed to be wise, writes Ursula Le Guin—please don't pronounce her name [lœ:gwin]. And they are allowed to be cute. Quaint. Feisty. Spry, she adds. The day's looking up. Rise. Move. I used to be an aerialist. Walked on my hands. Hung from hoops and swings. Until a fixed doubles trapeze act catapulted me from cloud swing to stratus, cumulus congestus, cirrostratus, cirrocumulus, cumulonimbus. Thunderhead. Squall. Lightning. Ka-BOOM. In rehabilitation I learned that every clown face is a variation of three basic types: *whiteface, auguste* and *character*. I put my energy into becoming me: a scarred comic harlequin. Now I stroll around the circus arena come tax time. Pause. A stop-act for the lions. Call me Scar.

I've met him. Tick. Tock. He casts a big shadow with comments that cartwheel in black clouds of leaping frogs heading to the river. Ticky-tock-tock. My question—supposed to be wise—tumbles forty minutes in a back road, then: what's the deal with the river? He looks like death warming up, his teeth darkly stained by chromogenic bacteria that no paste could erase, not from that crowded dentition, no. Lemony Snicket, he says, you ask all the wrong questions. If you can't see it, you can't say it. You seek to tackle the issue of clowns falling out of a hearse, and that's a series of unfortunate events.

Dark energy

A thwack. You sink into yourself. An explosion of elementary particles. You are a supernova shooting through air and stars. A baryonic ball of bleeding energy scattering matter in the void. Your heart beats out of place like wind gusting on a high plain. Pulse hovers on a knife edge. You wriggle out of your body. Crawl through gaseous clouds to a rocky alcove they call emergency. Climb the lookout they call a chair. Fall into antigravity. Whizz through a constellation of voices eying your soul from the back of beyond. When you come to, Nurse Adani tells you not to touch your stitches. Or it will scar. You take your eyes off her badge. Stare at her face as though through a telescope. This is what a black hole looks like in a spark chamber.

Cusp. It's a noun. A fold or flap of a cardiac valve, but some-thing is about to change. You become an ocean smothered with grief, swelling and wailing as you escape the ordinary, lurching between scars and poverty beneath a dawn-tinted moon lit in such terrible taste. A supernova hurtles across your tide, no ending in sight.

The metaphysicist at the waterfront police station

The name is Man Ray, after the photographer. I was born in the air the day Akhenaton offered his first rayograph to the sun. I'm not a psychopath. I just strike transparent surfaces and bounce off them. Reflect, refract, diffuse, disperse. It's risky business all that cutting. Tiring not to think in a straight line. Scary to travel sideways. No sense of direction and therefore not an aficionado of Descartes. I'd say I'm closer to Pascal: I'm agoraphobic and prone to panic attacks. As for the scars, well, a few too many wavefront collisions. And no, I don't drink. Nor do I smoke.

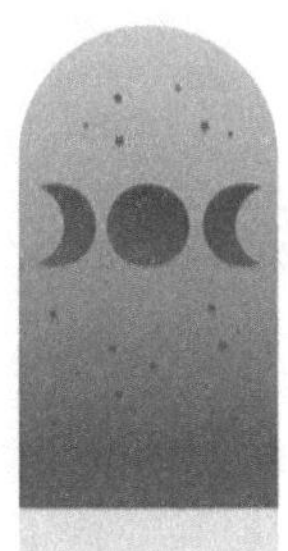

Your name is Petula, after the color of spring. You were born with a high decibel roar in a world of smoke that twirled faultless into the horizon. Everyone knew the plan, but you made it by a bee's eyelash. Your wholly shaken mother was out of her tree. You crawled out of sync to her breast, as she dispersed names in her delirium. Clarabo. Clarey. Cloggywogs. What now? Reflection. Refraction. Diffusion. Dispersion. It's a risky business. Listening filled you with bile and all goodwill toward humanity soaked itself in leaves whose sound was a whisper of insects. Later you'd say you're closer to Gladiola: detached, no phobia of hurting people. And yes, you love belligerence. And homicide for profit.

Tears

Forget doomsday, pestilence, carnage, the mess of history, climate change and the nihilistic lure of post-apocalyptic catastrophes. Tears are a premonition of closing bookshops, prefiguring empty shelves, the impoverishment of writers, the total collapse of language and the incursions of dust and daylight. According to Madame Sossostris's retail forecast, it's sunlight and happiness on February 10th and we must burn the peacock feathers so that rainbow smoke smothers you and the many years of us.

In the years since we parted, first you were a thunderstorm, your lightning an electric whip. Then you were light rain, soaking but harmless. The day you became a tugging wind and all I needed was a long sleeve, I knew that soon you would be mist, distant in the horizon, like a premonition of closing bookshops. Empty shelves, it makes no difference being there. The silver and gold bracelet on the chiffonier—in a moment of irony, you gave me that? Oh, and the Sat Nav in my car, it serves me better than a thousand yous. If you knock quietly and open my door through your tears, I might give you a coin and an old shirt, or call the cops to a strange ghost. I carry a new sunlight full of rainbows in my belly. She will never be a memory of you.

Fear of sand

So many sandcastles collapsing at the ocean's edge as the day melts in the virtual time of lost childhoods. You shiver. Drop by drop an old wound weeps in your heart. The bitter taste of geranium in your mouth; its acrid scent lingers in the air. So many hallucinations in real time even as you gouge out ghostly images from your eyes, silence eerie voices in your ears and drown unspeakable fears in the rising tide. What follows is no unpredictable speculation, but the certainty of premonition: the Sandman is coming tonight.

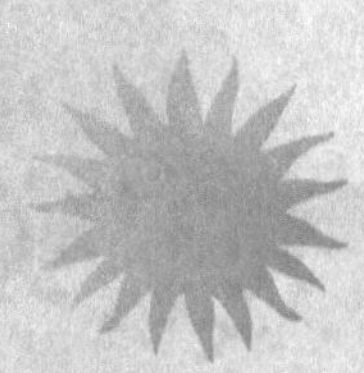

The sandcastle inside the collapsing beehive is a buzz hole full of licorice and it is black with hallucinations of lost childhood. Sigh by sigh, your blood spikes to stagger your heartbeat, as bees drink the extract of sweet root and you dip a finger in their bile. Must you grow wings before you stop licking the salt and sugar, both ghostly and aromatic, how so bitter yet so sweet? You try not to sleep, just dip a finger, dip a finger, what sort of fool says licorice, let's do it? Enough, enough. We keep watch in the castle but the day breaks and the sun rises low with a ditty of sand people effusive in their hugs and one of them is you.

Waterlogged

It's raining nicely between the floorboards—and by Jove we need water. But it's a sad story that you have inscribed on the woven floor-spread made of wool and animal hair in the mid-nineties in Baluchistan, Pakistan and well before you and all others met in folklore and further cultural revisions of yore. Well after, it's raining ropes. I could go up or down. Look where the line is fraying. Pick up where *It's raining nicely,* except the floorboards are water-logged. Way to go . . . Remember how we fought over "groupuscules"? Who speaks and acts? What for?

She is swimming between floorboards—it doesn't make sense
but, by Jove, it feels grave. Above her head is a carpet that is not
an environmental antiphon and a wonky table that will never
be a solid hold for the slippery slope of relationship ores—they
resurface with no regard of how grade, concentration and
occurrence directly affect the cost of mining the edge she needs
to restrain the fraying lines of what remains. Waterlogged. It's
a national emergency that will slip door after door after door
out of the apartment into a library on the beach and it's full
of books that howl there's no global crisis.

Blood and tears (if not too contentious)

We learn the taste of blood and tears in the womb. Whether it is the same salt I can't tell, though I suspect Samuel Becket would have answered in the positive. Now how timely that this week an exhibition titled "The Model Citizen" should open at our Institute's Gallery as the Australian Federal Government confirms that it will remove all refugee children from Nauru. These persistent issues of who is and is not Australian are creatively explored in what promises to be a compelling event curated by academics and artists, including Alexander Pope, a biomedical animator and poet who combines cinema, poetry and science to reveal the microscopic worlds inside our bodies. His work on blood and tears sits firmly within the accepted conception of model citizenship and marries scientific praxis with the arts. Not only is Pope our Institute's Chancellor and Head of Research, he is also chair of the Academy of the Humanities. Herewith, an excerpt from his latest work:

> Vice with such giant strides comes on amain,
> Invention strives to be before in vain;
> Feign what I will, and paint it e'er so strong,
> Some rising genius sins up to my song.
>
> —Alexander Pope, Epilogue to the Satires (1738), Dialogue II

Curiocity was a metropolis that escaped the lunch time routine. Animated osteos, plumbers, electricians, baristas, forecasters, novelists, hairdressers, and all, closed shop soon as the clock struck twelve. Buggy services, tickets and information booths sprung up every which way to guide folk to the next blood sale. No lock-in contracts or demands for passholders only, anyone was welcome who was keen to chase with giant strides in the direction of liquid plasma or solid red blood or white blood cells or platelets, or a mottled mass of all the above, consumed, inhaled, injected or drip-fed. Curiofolk religiously adored the Greek physician Galen who married philosophy with anatomy to understand that arteries carried blood. Everyone accepted the concept of Karl Landsteiner, who won the Nobel Prize in Physiology or Medicine in 1930 for his findings on ABO blood types, but they quite couldn't get it that he never became emperor of the universe. Leukocytes! yelled a hawker. Amino acids! yelled another, as three buggies collided at a T-junction where stunned traffic lights, mesmerized by the blood rush, had stalled. By two o'clock, everyone was back at their day job, model citizens with eyes open—perusing bones, drains, cables, espressos, heatwaves, excerpts and wigs. No one ever asked the government or rumored with the black market about where, oh, where, the fresh, sublime human blood came from.

A desperate vitality

No wind. No stars. No moon. Bodies of trees clustered close to the window of my fiction room mark the whims of weather, not the cycle of seasons. Oppressive heat. The stink of burning rubber. A night to match my mood. The fall when I saw the body being fished out from the creek . . . The friend who'd led me there had designs on my purse and so walked me away from the scene. We went to the pub. Had a beer. Failed to rekindle the conversation. And now Igor Stravinsky has just stolen my thunder. In the first of his Harvard lectures, he writes: "the meaning of poetics is the study of work to be done. The verb *poiein* from which the word is derived means nothing else but to *do or make*." That was one year I was conceived.

Unfinished poems cartwheel in the stars on a windless night. The morning sun sighs out a name that is a testament to the fiction of life in a cycle of seasons. Nyambuli—it means daughter of the goat. But she is a child of the gods who write weekend notes, and a muse of the gods who rekindle Mondays to Fridays. She is true to her name in timidity, curiosity, uncertainty—despite occasional fits of temper when she morphs into a faun. Her world is full of myths and lore, no wind, no stars, no moon. Just a pentagram of spells. She roams, a free spirit, each experience reborn. And the gods accept.

Endgame without ending

You too, once thought you were on top of your game. After the Titans of the University were defeated, you shared a hot desk on Mount Olympus with astronomists and astrophysicists who, unlike you, conducted their collaborative research behind the closed doors of their laboratories. Every third Friday of the month you would meet at the Pantheon, the space where all the vigorous discussions among the scientists and chief administrators took place. Then one fateful morning you packed your meager pack of books and moved to the foot of Mount Parnassus (the handful of linguists and historians and philosophers had long disappeared). Having embraced the principle of heterogeneity inscribed within the very ethos of Parnassus, you devoted yourself to a theater of dreams, visions, mirrors, smokescreens and metaphors where images replace imitations that generate specular emotional responses in a constant act of decreation to reveal the core of an encounter of the self with the other. Endgame without ending?

In terms of overall structure, he is a Titan who needs such attentiveness. The flow of logic in his paragraphs . . . the sentences are too long. You lose yourself in the detail, seek ethos in compatible typeface but get distracted fixing taglines. He's not a type family you understand. Variants of original typeface bring emphasis and distinction while keeping a cohesive look. But that's not him. There's a difference in his lines, a vigorousness in the extensions and letterforms. He's not meant for comfortable reading—what is the hierarchy of information! He's inscribed in colors and textures, sizes and spacing, exaggerated in triangles and points. You want to go back, you cannot go back, how a single moment caught the both of you one fateful night on a hot desk that walked into a come-we-stay. But paradox or conundrum, he is a patient one. It's a metaphor of imbalance, heterogeneity in bedding. Puppy eyes mid typeface compressed into ravenous lion font. Non-connecting scripts demand coffee on the go. The pen moist in your fingers anticipates a pure taste of text. He prefers casual scripts: maybe do it in the bus on the way to the library! The contraception of literature is an endgame inscribed in your pocket.

acknowledgments

A big thank you to the distinguished members of the Prose Poetry Project run by the University of Canberra, led by Professor Paul Hetherington, and the enchantment of words shared in a safe but addictive environment that emboldened the linguistics and audaciousness of our speculative compositions.

about the authors

Dominique Hecq, MA, Dip Ed, PhD, worked as Research Leader in her capacity as Associate Professor in Writing at Swinburne University of Technology after teaching at a number of universities in Australia and overseas. She has a background in Literature as well as French and Germanic languages, with qualifications in translating. Hecq writes across disciplines, and sometimes across tongues. Her creative works comprise one novel, three collections of short stories, ten books of poetry and two one-act plays. She co-edited *Female Sexuality: The Early Psychoanalytic Controversies* (1998; 2015) and *Creative Writing with Critical Theory: Inhabitation* (2018), edited *The Creativity Market: Creative Writing in the 21st Century* (2013) and wrote the widely acclaimed *Towards a Poetics of Creative Writing* (2015). *Kaosmos* (2020) and *Tracks* (2020) are her most recent publications in English. Among her multiple awards for fiction, poetry and translation, Hecq is a recipient of the 2018 International Best Poets Prize administered by the International Poetry Translation and Research Centre in conjunction with the International Academy of Arts and Letters.

Eugen Bacon, MA, MSc, PhD, is African Australian, a computer scientist mentally re-engineered into creative writing. She's the author of *Claiming T-Mo* (Meerkat Press) and *Writing Speculative Fiction* (Macmillan). Her work has won, been shortlisted, longlisted or commended in national and international awards, including the Bridport Prize, Copyright Agency Prize, Australian Shadows Awards, Ditmar Awards and Nommo Award for Speculative Fiction by Africans. Eugen is a recipient of the Katharine Susannah Prichard (KSP) Emerging Writer-in-Residence 2021. Her creative work has appeared in literary and speculative fiction publications worldwide, including *Award Winning Australian Writing, Aurealis, Bards and Sages, Meniscus, TEXT Journal, Unsung Stories*, British Science Fiction Association's *Vector Magazine* and through Routledge in *New Writing*. In 2020 she released *The Road to Woop Woop and Other Stories* (Meerkat Press), *Hadithi & The State of Black Speculative Fiction* (Luna Press Publishing), *Ivory's Story* (NewCon Press) and *Black Moon* (IFWG).

Did you enjoy this book?

If so, word-of-mouth recommendations and online reviews are critical to the success of any book, so we hope you'll tell your friends about it and consider leaving a review at your favorite book-seller's or library's website.

Visit us at www.meerkatpress.com for our full catalog.

Meerkat Press
Atlanta